100 days, 100 GRAND

"**How to do healthcare**" second UK edition 2019

First published in Great Britain in 2019 by Redpump Ltd. Copyright © Chris Worth 2019.

The right of Chris Worth to be identified as the author of this work is asserted with all rights reserved.

This print perfect bound edition of "How to do healthcare" is **ISBN 978-1-912795-27-7**

See 100days100grand.com

"First, do no harm."

—Hippocrates, father of
modern medicine

"I stuffed their mouths with gold."

—NHS founder Nye Bevan,

on persuading doctors

I'm not a doctor. Or a health pundit. Or a politician. I'm not even sick.

So why am I—a freelance writer with a bit of b-school savvy—claiming the right to tell you what's wrong with healthcare?

Simply: because I've *studied the system and noted its problems*. Not from the emotional viewpoint of caring for a sick relative, or having my life saved by a guy in a white coat. But on the *numbers* and *evidence* that, together, provide the big picture.

And that big picture shows: almost everywhere it's practiced, healthcare is done wrong.

Why is it such a money sink, outpacing inflation the world over? *Why* are outcomes so slow to improve, even as budgets spiral? *Why* are patients seen as problems to be dealt with, not customers to be served? And *what*, in an ideal world, would we do about it?

This book starts by defining the three Big Problems of healthcare, with the emotional and financial factors driving them. It then looks at their effects in context, and demonstrates why change at the edges can't work.

Then—on the basis problems are useless without solutions—it proposes a model for sustainable, affordable, quality healthcare for all, and a six-point plan for introducing it.

Let's start our diagnosis.

CHRIS WORTH

WHAT IS HEALTHCARE?

Healthcare is healing the sick, mending the wounded, and preventing disease from killing you.

At least, that's what it *should* be.

Almost everywhere, it's anything but.

Paid for principally by national budgets, healthcare is a political hot potato, gamed by providers and owned by activists. Wherever you look, it's packed with entrenched interests and unintended consequences that, for the most part, lead to negative second-order effects for the person who matters: the patient.

All these issues have a common factor: **government**. Which is a shame, because what healthcare should *not* be is a government service.

But—and this is the reason for this little book—there's an alternative approach that can solve these issues, *and* take us from where we are now to where we want to be. Even better, it's an approach that sees the issues as *opportunities*, not intractable problems.

It's a view that returns healthcare to its Hippocratic origins, albeit with fewer leeches: a trusted transaction between patient and provider, without politicians telling you how you "should" do it.

Above all, it takes the position that the patient is not the problem. The patient is the *solution*.

Come now. This won't hurt a bit.

HEALTHCARE IS A PROFESSIONAL SERVICE

Because being sick is an emotive subject, many people see healthcare as some sort of human right.

This worldview is wrong. And it's the first of three Big Problems blocking the way forward.

One rebuff is philosophical: nothing can be a "right" if it involves forcing someone else to do something for you, like provide medical care. But the real argument here is *practical*.

Healthcare is delivered by experts with years of training. It needs buildings, equipment, systems, processes. *Infrastructure* that needs a strategic plan and investment capital. This takes *work*.

Which makes healthcare an economic activity. A matter of value created and exchanged. Of *business*.

This means healthcare is a *professional service*, no different in principle to taxi driving or accountancy.

Most (not all) of healthcare's problems, worldwide, stem from denial of this basic truth. Pretending healthcare is a gift from gods or governments—an *entitlement*, to be provided free of charge without limit—is what led to the immense distortions that characterise healthcare worldwide.

But once we accept healthcare is a professional service—not a great leap, really—there are workable solutions. Actually, *great* solutions.

So the first step in doing healthcare is to let it be

what it is: **a business**. Skilled people offering their talents to those who want them, where success comes from satisfying customers and offering better products and services at competitive prices.

(Isn't that what we all want—higher quality, greater value, providers competing to attract your custom?)

But before exploring solutions, let's look at the reasons so many people believe healthcare *is* a right. These beliefs are not "stupid". They're just overly subjective, distorted by politics and personal experience. We can sum them up as public perception, government overreach, and the nature of health.

First things first: **public perception**, and what drives the most toxic narrative in all of healthcare.

1. THE TOXIC BELIEF

Put simply, the reason so many think healthcare *is* a right is that it's mostly paid for by government. Which makes it feel free. And "rights" are things you don't have to pay for . . . right?

Of course, healthcare is anything but free.

The UK's NHS costs the equivalent of £4,600 a year per household. Germany's social insurance setup sucks 8% of your salary, and it's compulsory. France charges 5.25%, and only covers 70% of the costs. Canada's system gorges US$200bn, and it's *illegal* for a private hospital to compete with a government one. And let's not even start on the USA's Medicare and Medicaid, which gulp a staggering $1.3 *trillion*.

In short, far from being free, healthcare is very *expensive*. So the perception is that government must provide it, since the average citizen can't afford it.

(And if the only example of a "private" healthcare system you have is the USA—whose hyper-gamed non-market is a mess—this sounds perfectly reasonable.)

So to break this toxic ideology—that healthcare is a human right and must be guaranteed by government—we need deeper insight into what drives it.

The reasons are threefold. One is a phenomenon called **local optima**, magnified by a typical outcome of government provision: the **absence of options**. Both are abetted by **Prospect Theory**.

1a. Prospect Theory stymies improvement

Discovered by Daniel Kahnemann, <mark>Prospect Theory</mark> illustrates how people place more value on what's here and now than what they could get in the future.

This is understandable. The present is certain, the future less so. (And hence, less valuable.) The pointy bit is that people *overweight the present*.

As the psychological value—the feel-good factor—of something rises, so does its monetary value . . . only not as fast.

(See the graph next page. For each unit rise in the psychological value of a thing, its perceived value in *monetary* terms rises less.)

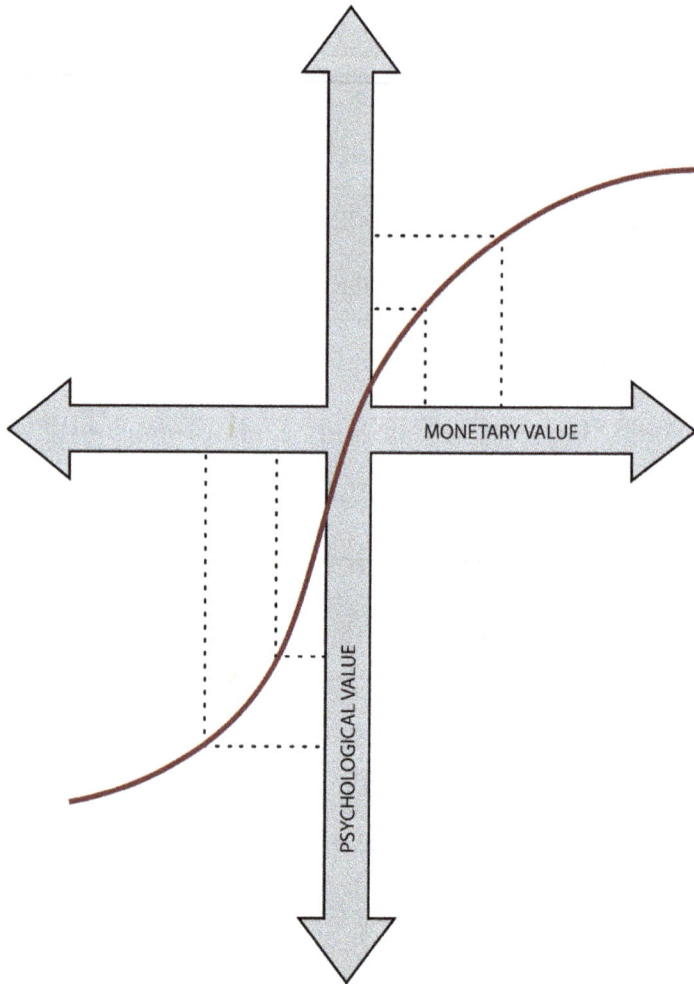

MONETARY VALUE

PSYCHOLOGICAL VALUE

In other words, the more invested you feel in what you've already got—like Britain's cradle-to-grave NHS—the less likely you are to consider alternatives.

This is a core reason so many people worldwide support government-provided healthcare. It's what they've got now, and the benefits of any other system feel distant.

This outcome of Prospect Theory is exacerbated by the problem of **local optima**, up next.

1b. Local optima blind us to better

Say you want to scale the highest peak in the Himalayas. You're standing next to it right now: it looks *huge*. Bigger than any other. So you climb up and take your selfie.

But from your new viewpoint, it's clear you're not on the highest peak at all. In fact, there are quite a few higher ones in the distance. However, to scale those higher peaks, you've got to go down *your* hill first, and lose what you've achieved so far.

You can't see an easy route from here to there. And the sun's low in the sky, you're a bit tired, and it'll soon be too dark for Instagramming.

So you resolve to stay on your current summit. In fact, you wonder if you could somehow make your current hill *taller* instead.

That's a local optima. Not the best, but the best you could see when you started out. But abandoning a local optima in the search for a better one (like the *global* optima, the one that's best of all) **carries a cost**. And thanks to Prospect Theory, you value the peak beneath your feet more than the distant, taller one anyway.

That's why public healthcare, no matter how bad, seems so entrenched. Systems like Britain's NHS are a local optima, and it's a big problem for people to see beyond them.

1c. Absence of options prevents us thinking

It's even harder to see a distant peak when the sky's too cloudy. In fact, when there's a scarcity of visible options, even *thinking* about other possibilities feels somehow not-the-done-thing.

This is the situation in the UK, where private health spending is a tiny 2% segment of the total. Many people—born in their local hospital, known to their local GP (family doctor)—are only vaguely aware it even *exists*, despite insurance cover being highly competitive. It's hard to compete against "free".

But it's not just the UK. In the USA, the Affordable Care Act ("Obamacare") mandated high coverage for low prices, making the market unattractive. Whole states ended up with just one ACA-approved health plan; some had *none*. That's hardly consumer choice.

You can't demonstrate the superiority of other approaches to people who've never experienced them.

So pointing out that higher peak, in itself, won't change anyone's mind. With government healthcare occupying so much share-of-mind, many people don't even accept other options have a right to *exist*.

Which means any shakeup in healthcare has to be broad and gradual, with consumer benefits at every step—not a scorched-earth approach starting over from zero. (However much fun that'd be.)

You don't get people on board by threatening their way of life—and in the UK, the NHS is more state religion than healthcare provider. Opposing it in any way whatsoever will bring angry mobs to your house wielding pitchforks. (Yes, public perception is that ingrained.)

Luckily, broad, gradual, non-threatening change is precisely the *right* way to solve all three Big Problems in healthcare, plus the pitchfork one. So that's the approach our proposed solution will take later.

But for now, with the first Big Problem—**the toxic belief**—and its three drivers in mind, let's move on to the second: **government overreach**.

2. UNNATURAL MONOPOLIES

Once upon a time, the common view was that certain services were "natural monopolies": business sectors where competition was unhelpfully predatory and wasteful. Because a town only needs one telephone company, or energy provider, or railway line, right?

However laughable it sounds, this remains the view across much of the world's public sector.

But in a functioning ecosystem—and that includes anywhere value is exchanged between providers and consumers, like an economy—predators and competition are *good*. As prey, you're forced to improve, or end up as lunch. The strongest, fittest individuals survive to breed a stronger, fitter next generation. It's a process of continuous improvement: no time to get fat or lazy.

Government has no natural predators. So when it provides healthcare, it tends to gets slower. Fatter. Less fit. And that's our second Big Problem in healthcare: government overreach.

There's a place for government, of course. Its purpose is to protect your individual rights, so you can live your life without fear. But when government provides you with services that *aren't* rights, like healthcare, its advantage of being the sole authority becomes a huge *dis*advantage for citizens.

Why? Because it has no incentive to improve . . . and a professional service *should* have such incentives.

As with public perception, three factors drive this. One is what we'll call the medical-industrial complex: government's inbuilt tendency to favour insiders and seek monopolies, like any other organisation. (It's Prospect Theory at the organisational level.) Following it comes the inexorable growth that results from the incentive to get bigger rather than better. (It's the flipside of local optima.) And where public perception was shaped by an absence of *options*, government's absence of *competition* tends to produce a subpar product at an superpar price: mediocrity at a premium. (Why bother raising your bar, if there's nobody else around raising theirs?)

Let's take a look at these three driving factors of the second Big Problem in healthcare.

2a. The medical-industrial complex

It's odd how those most passionately against "private monopolies" like Google and Facebook tend to fully favour *government* monopolies in sectors like schools and healthcare. This contradiction is because they mix up the two *types* of monopoly: ==coercive and competitive==.

Microsoft was a monopoly in its time, yet nobody worries about it now. Google arguably remains one, yet started losing engineers the day Facebook—not even in the same sector—hit browsers.

Now, Facebook is seen as old school, and the kids get their social fixes elsewhere. All these companies invest huge sums in winning and retaining customers; all have grown the broader economy.

They are *competitive monopolies*. A player can only become a market leader by providing products and services that people value. The moment a competitor innovates with something they value more, that monopoly fades away.

Contrast this to sectors like the law, schools . . . and healthcare.

New entrants need to jump through endless hoops while wrapped in red tape. Competition is artificially constrained; innovation makes a snail look snappy; benefits accrue to insiders able to play the system.

These are *coercive monopolies*. Sectors that protect their positions not by providing goods and services customers value, but by lobbying and laws.

Most coercive monopolies are in sectors with heavy government involvement. Most competitive monopolies are not.

In much of the West, of course, healthcare is the most coercive monopoly of all. Similar to the *military-*industrial complex—a tacit pact between government insiders and connected contractors to keep money flowing to a favoured few—it's a *medical*-industrial one, inward-looking and focussed on getting bigger rather than better.

(This explains why the solution offered so often for dysfunctional healthcare is "single-payer"—in other words, making it a government monopoly. Guess which alliance of interests is behind *those* efforts?)

This matters, because no coercive monopoly ever delivered a quality product, much less continuous improvement. Nationalised industries *always* lead to lower output, poorer services, and worse outcomes. Because customer satisfaction is not their critical success factor; striving for it is not in their nature.

(Note the drivers of coercive monopolies are at the organisational level, not the personal. Many people actually *providing* public sector healthcare are caring and hardworking. Organisational factors aren't any fault of Matron.)

Accordingly, coercive monopolies are one driver of our second Big Problem. Let's look at another.

2b. Inexorable growth

Many in government deride "the market" and see their own approach as superior. Which is odd, because public sector organisations behave *exactly* as any private sector player would. They seek to control resources, grow their influence, and raise barriers to entry against competitors.

Which is why coercive monopolies tend to grow, grow, grow.

When you have no incentive to get *better*, you get very good at getting *bigger*.

The USA's healthcare budget grows 4-6% a year despite inflation of under 2%; it approaches 20% of

GDP. The UK's NHS is the fifth-largest employer in the world, spends 10% of its £120bn+ budget on conditions arising from *overeating*, and forks out £3 for your 44p packet of aspirin. Yet the cries never end: *more government funding*.

And politicians come up with more ways to spend taxpayer money, year after year. (Often with public approval.) Of course, this lets them get bigger still.

Such tendencies happen in the private sector too. But there's a difference. The private sector is open to competition and innovation, and even entrenched players can get squished like a bug.

Of 500 firms on Fortune's list of the biggest global corporations in 1955, just 60 were still there the same number of years later; turnover per decade was over 40%. Yes: even being the biggest gave you a barely 50:50 chance of remaining so for ten years.

By contrast, government departments tend to stick around, outlasting administrations and electoral cycles alike. Economics is red in tooth and claw; government provision of healthcare, sadly, isn't.

This is another factor in our second Big Problem: without any brake on their behaviour, government-financed healthcare systems tend to get bigger and build that unnatural, coercive monopoly.

Let's look at the last factor in government overreach: its incessant **mediocrity**.

2c. Mediocrity at a premium

In the old Soviet Union, government planners thought consumer goods should be produced by the State. Lucky denizens of the worker's paradise could buy cardboard-tipped cigarettes, or televisions with a 70% DOA rate, or join a years-long waiting list for a rotbucket car called a Lada.

In short: **the products were shit**.

(And despite their laughable quality, they weren't cheap, either. A Lada would cost many times a worker's salary.)

Communism provides the most amusing examples, but in fact this mediocrity-at-a-premium is a hallmark of *any* government-provided service. ("Good enough for government work" has been the sigh of contractors for decades.)

UK public hospitals are a cacophony of queues and crowds; a waiting time of four hours for emergency treatment is the *target*, still missed for one in ten patients. The average GP limits consultations to ten minutes. The NHS's crumbling wards offer fewer acute beds per head than almost any Western country, and occupancy exceeds 95% most winters.

This doesn't mean government planners are incompetent. (And certainly not the average A&E worker.) They're just conflicted. You can't produce great consumer products if you're not driven by consumer desires.

This is the third factor against government overreach: *the product always ends up substandard, yet costly*.

Combined with the tendency towards coercive monopolies and inexorable growth, it's clear this second Big Problem—**government overreach**—is, if anything, even harder to solve than our first, **public perception**.

But before we start looking at solutions, let's throw a third Big Problem into this devil's cocktail: healthcare's **Methuselah Complex**.

3. THE METHUSALEH COMPLEX

With more healthcare, people live longer. When people live longer, they need more healthcare. And when people lead longer, healthier lives, they want healthcare to solve ever-smaller health issues. (Especially if it's "free".)

Contrary to popular myth, if you take out infant mortality active lifespans haven't increased much in the last few centuries. (And in the USA, they're arguably going down.) But *inactive* lifespans have. The average Brit suffers seven years of ill health in life's last act. And First World problems like poor posture, obesity, and mental illness are ever more widespread.

This is the third Big Problem of healthcare: demand

begets demand.

In any private business, this isn't a problem at all. Customers wanting more of what you sell is *success*. But government's tendency to get bigger and exclude competitors turns this silk purse into a pig's ear.

Again, this third Big Problem of healthcare has three parts. Let's look at overuse, scope creep, and the elastic norm in turn.

3a. A common tragedy

When you provide something for free, it encourages people to get as big a chunk of it as possible. This is one of three contributing factors to healthcare's demand problem: **overuse**.

Of course, overuse isn't limited to healthcare. And certainly not to the public sector. Ocean fisheries, forest plantations, oil extraction: all are distorted by the perception a resource is free, with the incentive to take as much of it as you can get.

Now healthcare isn't a tract of land. But it suffers from this **tragedy of the commons** just the same. When you offer people free stuff, they *take* free stuff.

Greece's ex-finance minister Yanis Varoufakis claims you "can't put a price on healthcare". In other words, healthcare must be free and open to all, in limitless quantity, forever, whatever the cost. Similar pronouncements stem from American and British politicians. This is, of course, nonsense.

(Such beliefs drove Greece's long-brewing economic crash around 2009.)

The first principle of economics (which Varoufakis supposedly studied) is that **all resources are scarce**. Healthcare is not different just because it involves saving lives. Hospitals need maintaining. Surgeons need equipment. Nurses need salaries.

Maybe you can't put a *value* on healthcare. To a

person with cataracts, the value of being able to see again is incalculable. But healthcare absolutely *does* have a price.

In fact, with the right approach, that price is surprisingly easy to find.

So doing healthcare right means it cannot be treated as a commons. We'll explore alternatives soon. But next, let's look at **scope creep**.

3b. The creeping of the scope

The NHS was never intended to serve waiting rooms full of sniffling adults. Yet it now does, despite a cure for the common cold remaining elusive. At weekends, A&E departments overflow with alcohol-related injuries; shocking sums are poured into self-inflicted conditions. Obesity's reversible and preventable consequences—like Type II Diabetes—add up to an incredible 20% of all spending.

On the continent, Germany pays for hundreds of thousands of homeopathic (aka "useless") remedies every year; so, until 2017, did the UK. French doctors prescribe pills and potions for tired legs and minor aches across the shoulders.

As we've seen, when you hold a coercive monopoly, the way to increase your power and influence is to grow bigger. So it's not surprising nationalised healthcare systems are constantly finding and treating new conditions. Meeting demand just increases demand.

This is the biggest factor in healthcare costs: the rare condition that sucks in disproportionate resource, the minor ailment that steals expensive hours from someone with ten years of training. To do healthcare right, scope creep must stop . . . or at least be *properly priced*.

Finally, on to the third (and related) factor in our third Big Problem: **the elastic norm**.

3c. The elastic norm

At face value, we're a lot sicker than we used to be.

American psychiatry's standard reference, the *Diagnostic and Statistical Manual of Mental Disorders*, grew from 134 to 494 pages between 1950 and 1980; it's now at 1,000. The UK codes for 92,000+ types of clinical interaction, and its 66m people consume 19m of them each year in hospitals . . . *excluding* emergency treatment (23m) and everyday doctor's visits (300m). The average Japanese heads for the *ishi* 13 times a year. Even in the USA, subject to budget-busting market distortions, the doc's is a quarterly event.

Yes, we're sick. But not *that* sick.

What's happening here is a change in your ==normatives==. The healthier you are, the higher your *definition* of healthiness ratchets up . . . and the more you feel your little aches and pains need treatment, rather than a night's sleep. (Every British GP has her cast of well-but-worried "regulars".)

This Methusaleh issue—endless demand, limitless coverage, costs without end—is the third Big Problem of healthcare, combining overuse, scope creep, and the elastic norm. As you can see, they're all related.

But enough driving factors. With our Big Problems defined, let's look next at their big *outcomes*.

MALIGN MISALIGNMENTS

In one UK hospital, consultants raised a patient safety issue. Each patient required x amount of time, they argued: more than 8 patients per session would be risky. They were paid £600 per session. (The consultants, not the patients.)

A private hospital opened next door, and offered those same professionals similar work—with one difference. They'd be paid *per patient*, not a day rate.

Magically, 8 patients stopped being a limit. It became "safe" to see 10,12, even 16 patients in one day. (Legends tell of one who managed 20.)

Also in the UK, family doctors receive a set sum per

patient registered with them, around £150. Per *year*, not per visit. In other words, the more you can keep a patient out of your consulting room, the higher your profit. Yet some wonder why it can be hard to get an appointment.

For many years, NHS dentistry funded dentists per-procedure, rather than on maintaining oral health. The dentists themselves got to decide when a procedure was due. Goldmine! Why tell the guy in the chair all he needs is better brushing, when you could earn £100 in the next 15 minutes drilling and filling?

This is the problem with all public (and a fair bit of private) healthcare: *misaligned incentives.*

Some pundits claim healthcare is "special", "not

driven by economics". Which is total bullshit.

As we've established, healthcare is a professional service, a business like any other. In fact, these misaligned incentives *prove* it.

After all, people tend to act in their own best interests. And medical professionals are no different. More to the point: there's nothing *wrong* with such behaviour. It's human nature.

The *system* is at fault, not the people. Because it's **gameable**. How misalignments lead to system-gaming is the next part of understanding what's wrong with healthcare . . . and what's key to doing it right.

THE GAMEABLE CHARADE

When rewards stem from a score or metric rather than the intended outcome, the incentive is to focus on the metric. It's called "gaming the system".

Slathered in metrics and targets, healthcare is as gameable as it gets.

According to government measures, one British hospital was getting patients in and out in record time. It turned out to be "storing" patients in ambulances outside, since the clock only started ticking once the gurney crossed the threshold. It gamed the system.

Recognising overcrowding in A&E departments, the British government introduced SDECs: stopgap clinics between the emergency room and a hospital bed. However, a patient sent to a SDEC from an A&E would drop off the A&E's To-Do list. So when waiting times drifted towards the targeted four hours, a lot of patients got referred to an SDEC. Because for the A&E staff, that was a way to meet the metric.

(This isn't a dig at A&E staff. They face serious consequences for missing metrics. So if the metric can be gamed without harming the patient, you go for it.)

Government inspectors rightly want to know when a hospital's death rate rises above average. For fairness, their metric excluded end-of-life care, since patients in palliative are *expected* to die. After this metric was introduced, there was a bump in people dying *in* palliative who hadn't originally been admitted *to* it.

(In brief: if you didn't want an extra death on your numbers, you sent 'em to the palliative ward to draw their last breath.)

This gameable charade isn't limited to government: it happens in all organisations of any size, anywhere. But it's most *common* in government, because government is bigger and more complex. The more complicated any system of rewards, the more potential it has to be gamed.

But relax. Incentives aren't the problem so much as the *solution*. Let's see why.

. . . AND HOW TO FIX IT

Doctors doctoring documents, nurses doing naughties in the night. Does that make the average hospital a hotbed of collusion, crime, and calumny?

It does not—in the slightest. It's just human beings, doing what human nature demands. So is there any good news?

Actually, this *is* the good news.

Let's get past "bad" and "good" incentives for a moment, to the deeper truth: **incentives work**.

Find a way to get those incentives aligned in the best interests of all stakeholders, and the building blocks of high-quality healthcare all click into place.

We don't have to look far for the model: it exists already. And it's responsible for better products and services, greater customer choice and freedom, and the highest standards of living in history for the greatest number of people the world has ever known.

It's existed for centuries. Some call it the **System of the World**.

THE SYSTEM OF THE WORLD

There is one—and *only* one—economic motivator that produces continuous improvement in goods and services: the **profit incentive**.

There is one—and *only* one—way to make sure incentives align in the most beneficial way between providers and consumers: **market forces**.

And there is one—and *only*, well, guess the number— system of economic organisation that prevents coercive monopolies and lets innovation thrive: **free-market capitalism**.

Mention "profit" to many in British healthcare, and expect to see them shudder. But profit is *good*. In addition to being great for your credit rating, profits are a social signal: they're the purest way of telling you your products and services are valued by others.

Hospitals provide a valuable service. Which is why they should be profit-making businesses operating in a competitive market. (And, of course, paying taxes like everyone else.)

That's the route to our solution for healthcare: run it according to the long-proven System of the World, **free-market capitalism**.

As a thought experiment, forget your personal politics for a moment and consider where you would rather have lived in the last few decades:

Hardscrabble North Vietnam in the 1950s, or the

prosperous markets in the South? The People's Republic of China in the '60s, or booming Hong Kong and Taiwan? '70s East Berlin, or across the border in West Germany? 1980s Western Europe, or the Soviet satellites to the East? North or South Korea, today?

Management supremo Peter Drucker on the free market: *"It does not work too well, but nothing else works at all."*

The free market is a machine for discovering products and services people want, and rewarding those who provide them. It is *not* one alternative among equals, any more than Darwinian evolution is in the same sack as the various god theories.

And that's why it's our solution for healthcare.

"CHARITABLE STATUS"

Around about now, you're thinking of charities.

Many "private" hospitals operate as charities, don't they? And charity is good, isn't it? Couldn't charitable status solve healthcare's problems, removing it from the nasty red-in-tooth-and-clawness of capitalism?

In a word: **nope**.

By contrast, the profit motive exposes why medical providers should *never* enjoy that wretched perk called "charitable status".

Charitable status exempts a business from paying its share of taxes, giving it a free ride on public infrastructure. In brief, it provides a sneaky shortcut to greater profits, without the need for pesky things like competing or innovating. And since the managers of charities can't usually take those profits out for themselves, they're faced with the same perverse incentives as other public sector bodies: inexorable growth that smothers alternatives.

(This is another reason the USA's supposedly private healthcare market is in deep trouble.)

Charities are no more suitable for delivering healthcare than government entities. There is a *place* for them—as we'll see later—but it's not as providers.

Now that's sorted, back to the free market.

"I STUFFED THEIR MOUTHS WITH GOLD"

If you believe clinical professionals are saints and heroes unmoved by market incentives, refer to this quote. It was Health Minister Aneurin "Nye" Bevan's solution when the BMA (a trade union) opposed the setup of Britain's National Health Service.

Yes: the NHS exists because a politician bought off the doctors.

This is not a complaint that doctors are greedy, anti-social, money-grubbing power-peddlers. In fact, it's a *celebration* of them . . . for that same reason.

It is not a crime to want to be paid for what you do. Nor, if what you do is difficult and in demand, to be paid a *lot*.

Those who sweated over textbooks for years to acquire saleable skills deserve the maximum the market is prepared to pay as their reward.

So this is *not* a tirade against doctors. Far from any saintly notion of public service, the NHS only *exists* because doctors considered it a good business proposition . . . and a canny politician recognised it.

That's why healthcare needs to be a free market. With a business model that allows low cost access to high quality treatments, and pays providers the proper market price at all times.

That business model is **insurance**, up next. But not health insurance as you know it.

REASSURING INSURANCE

Insurance gets a bad rep, particularly if you live amid the healthcare-hopelessness of the USA.

What's important to note is that the USA's failings—massive expense, extreme complexity, opaque pricing structures—are due to government interference, not any failure of the insurance model itself.

Subject to strictures and metrics, health insurance is as gameable as any socialised health system. That's why our model for healthcare isn't health insurance as we know it. (And certainly not the US variety.)

It's *car* insurance.

The healthcare model in your garage

Before we look at car *insurance*, let's look at how people buy *cars*.

Your car may be a low-cost, low-mileage runabout, taking you to the shops for a decade plus. It may be a vital work tool, getting you to and fro between clients: you'll change it next year. Or it may be a treasured possession, taking up most of your spare cash but returning a lot of pleasure.

Here's the point: how you consume the driving experience is *your* choice to make. Not some "National Car Service" that sees driving as a human right to be provided free of charge to all.

There's a cheap and safe 1.3L hatchback. A sturdy and reliable white van. Or a beautiful brute with twin turbos and a spoiler the size of California.

Carmakers invest billions every year in winning you as a customer, by making cars for every purpose imaginable. And they do this within a market that's far from free; the auto industry is heavily regulated. But somehow they manage to make products people want to buy.

Because dealers want your business, and there are many of them—it's a competitive market—you can also get great *prices* for these four-wheeled wonders. In fact, there are some real bargains out there. If you're not concerned about appearances, a perfectly functional secondhand Hyundai might cost less than a month's salary. If you think your car defines your identity (more fool you) you'll pay over the odds for that new-car smell, perhaps leveraging your buying power with financing. And there's excellent information to help you make your choice: you can check out thousands of vehicles and prices on the web.

In short, the auto industry is everything hospitals should be. Market-driven, transparently priced, with deals and offers available to sweeten the transaction. A savvy shopper can get a *tremendous* deal.

You might think this can't apply to healthcare. Yet many hospitals actually *do* work this way.

Bangkok's Bumrungrad Hospital is *superlative*, with prices far below those in the West. (It actively markets to Westerners.) In the USA, a initiative called Direct Primary Care cuts out mountains of paperwork, with doctors charging patients a monthly subscription fee; many find the fee lower than medical insurance. In the UK, the (few) private GPs offer appointments within two hours or even walk-ins at reasonable rates, a far superior service to the local NHS GP.

And perhaps the biggest piece of evidence giving the lie to healthcare being "special" is *cosmetic* surgery.

Rarely available in socialised medicine, customers have to fork out for their nips and tucks from their own pockets. Because it's a transaction between buyer and seller in a competitive market, with both sides looking to maximise their benefit, prices have gone down consistently as the sector has grown, with providers offering deals and financing. Just like car dealers, but with scalpels.

These methods of serving customers can't *help* but be better than government efforts, because this is what the free market does. The price mechanism shows customers what they can afford, tells marketers what customers value, and encourages the investment that leads to greater customer satisfaction.

Now to why motor *insurance* is the ideal model, too.

The certainty of risk

To see why car insurance provides a model for healthcare, think of *why* you insure your vehicle. (Aside from the obvious legal requirement.) It's **risk**.

You don't expect your insurance to cover your annual MOT check. Or the monthly carwash, or new tyres. Much less keep your tank topped up. These are *predictable* and *expected* costs. You budget for them as normal costs of ownership.

If you don't want to pay them, there are options there too. You can drive less, to reduce wear-and-tear. You can take it easier on the corners, or "forget" to name your lead-footed daughter on the policy.

In other words, based on your personal situation, *you make choices that match the costs of your car with the value you get from it*.

Imagine if you *could* buy insurance that covered fuel and tyres. The premiums would be *huge*. And the deductible you'd have to agree to—let's call it a "co-pay"—would make it not worth it.

That's why fuel coverage isn't available in the insurance market, because it isn't a good business proposition for any stakeholder.

So what *do* you buy insurance for? Simple: you buy it to cover rare, ruinous, and unpredictable events.

You accept responsibility for filling up; the minor risk of running out of fuel isn't big enough to insure against. You accept that a ding in the car park comes out of your pocket. These aren't life-changing events.

But you *do* want some backup if you leave the office to find your SUV under a forty-tonne truck. Or if you get sued for causing an accident. Or if someone rams your car at 100km/h with you in it.

This is how insurers stay in business. Statistics show how often these rare, ruinous, and hard-to-predict events occur, letting insurers set premiums based on how likely they are to happen to *you*.

(If this sounds unpleasantly cold and clinical, try starting an insurance business *not* based on such principles and see how long you last.)

This is why a young male pays £4,000 for his car

insurance: statistically, his hot hatch will be in the wrecker's yard in three years. His Auntie Mildred, by contrast, pays £20 a month for her stock Toyota.

However, the insurer can't charge *unreasonable* premiums, because car insurance is a *very* competitive market. Customers can take their money elsewhere. Because of this competition, *everyone has options*, without any price-gouging regulations needed.

A teenage footballer can insure an £80,000 Bentley, *if he values it enough*. A man on six figures may drive a decade-old hatchback because the premiums are cheap. Everyone can choose higher or lower coverage, *depending on their personal situation*.

This is why motor insurance provides the ideal

model for health provision. Because it recognises the System of the World's wonderful trinity: the profit motive, market forces, and free-market capitalism. The way of doing things that keeps prices competitive, satisfies customer demand, and constantly innovates to improve products and services.

Of course, the motor insurance market is far from perfect. No market ever is. But while still stuffed with small print, car insurance *works*. Because it covers what insurance is supposed to cover: the life-changing bits. Not everything under the sun.

Now let's see how the car insurance model can apply to healthcare.

The plurality of options

When you think about it, your health is a lot like owning a car. You accept you're responsible for it. You take actions that keep it functional (like going to the gym). And you use it with an awareness of the risks involved.

Because you know if you *don't* do these things, it's going to cost you.

That's why the car insurance model is ideal for healthcare: it takes as a given that insurance shouldn't cover everything and that people are capable of making their own decisions. Yet this is a concept *socialised* healthcare rarely recognises.

Everyone gets the odd headache. Everyone sneezes in sniffles season. These events aren't rare or ruinous, yet public healthcare often tries to cover them. Because there's political capital to be made by promising everything to everyone, regardless of who wants it, who uses it, or how much it costs.

Socialised healthcare is like Las Vegas without the glam: an all-you-can-eat buffet open 24 hours. And we all know what happens when we go to Vegas.

This means costs rise to the roof and reach for the sky. And the Magical Money Tree only exists in the minds of politicians—not economic reality.

So to adopt car insurance as a model for healthcare, there must be consequences for the consumer. Good as well as bad. (This already happens when socialised medicine meets reality with too solid a thud. The UK's NHS no longer covers weight loss surgery, accepting that eating too much is your own problem.)

When there are consequences to consider, consumers change their behaviour. And an efficient insurance market *prices* those consequences with great accuracy. Because it's their business to do so.

Existing private health insurance, like the UK's BUPA, offers a range of discounts to those who take care of themselves with gym memberships and regular checkups. Leading to a healthier, happier population that *needs* less healthcare.

Sounds like a plan.

THE WAY FORWARD: A SIX-POINT PLAN

The car insurance model—a great example of how the free market can operate efficiently even in a highly regulated environment—gives us a way forward. Since it shares space with what we need from healthcare: protection against rare and ruinous events, a broad and deep market of providers, competitive pricing and consumer choice.

So let's get practical. What *actions* are needed to turn theory into practice, and solve the three Big Problems of healthcare: **public perception**, **government overreach**, and **demand begetting demand**?

In fact, we've solved two already.

Problem 2—**government overreach**—was nipped in the bud the moment we saw healthcare as a professional service, not a public one. And Problem 3, **demand begetting demand**, is bid begone by a basic reality of capitalism: customer demand is an *opportunity*, not a problem, a market to be served and satisfied for profit. With factors like overuse and scope creep zapped by the checks and balances of the price mechanism, which teaches consumers the consequences of their actions.

So the biggest of our Big Problems is the first: the **toxic belief** that healthcare is somehow a "right", to be provided by government. Let's build a plan for dealing with that, starting with showing citizens the true cost of government healthcare.

1. Itemise everything, everywhere

Sunlight is the best disinfectant. (Relax, nurses: this isn't advice for ward cleaning schedules.) So the very first step in doing healthcare right is to show people *what government healthcare really costs*.

People tend to vote for increased public spending whenever politicians propose it ... *except when it's clear what it'll cost them*. So instead of a catch-all tax bill, every tax return should show how much of your salary went to the country's healthcare bill.

In the UK, it's equivalent to £4,000 per taxpayer. Roughly half of the UK's tax take comes from corporate and sales taxes, so let's call it £2,000 instead. (Just to be fair.)

The average UK income (including part-timers) is £29,000. Of which £5,750 is taken in taxes. So here's the basic itemisation, to be printed in red on every tax return: ==35% of your total tax bill goes on the NHS!== And you're still only funding half of it.

Even this blunt approach would cause a stir. Perhaps all the stir we need. But there's a lot more fun to be had on your payslip. If we consider that £2,000 a lump sum per taxpayer, it'll represent a far larger proportion of the tax bill for lower earners. Meaning the people who both support the NHS most strongly, yet have to be most careful with money, suddenly become aware of how much they're paying for it. This would defray the perception healthcare is "free" . . . and raise awareness that it's very, very *expensive*.

Next, we could split that £2,000 into the proportion spent on primary care (GP services, about £500) or self-inflicted conditions like Type II Diabetes (about £300.) People might start phoning their MPs when they truly understand how much they're paying for Aunt Hilda's cream bun addiction.

And if we start itemising the 50% of health services not paid for from income taxes on *other* receipts—like the VAT applied to most purchases—people start seeing how much government healthcare is costing them, everywhere, every time they go shopping.

Remember, we're not *changing* anything here. We're just itemising what things cost. And who could argue against giving consumers more information?

2. Switch to a charging model for GPs

In the UK, family doctors called GPs are the gatekeepers of healthcare, the source of referrals to specialists and hospitals. Few realise how much of this "public" service is actually private.

That friendly GP surgery providing NHS services? It's a private business. So are all dentists. Many specialist clinics. And virtually all consultants.

So our next step in doing healthcare is to let them be the private businesses they are . . . and let them charge a small sum for each visit. Say £3.

This will stop the overuse that plagues British GPs. There's also a way to stuff their mouths with gold:

continue paying them that £150 per registered patient per year they get already. Each £3 is gravy.

(There's an old economic principle that when you give something away, you destroy its value. Even a nominal sum, like £3, avoids this. Don't we agree doctors are valuable? Great. Let's pay them.)

But time-limit that £150, with a clear deadline:

Dear GP, you've got another four years of your current contract . . . but then you're on your own.

The doctor is free to *not* charge that £3, of course. That's her prerogative, as a private business. But those not retiring in the next few years have an incentive to build up the "cash payer" part of their businesses rather than just trouser all those pound coins.

And how do they do that? By doing what any private business *should* do: *attract more customers*. Treat patients as the business growth opportunity they are.

Let's face it, £3 is still a huge bargain for meeting a professional with years of training—and with the cost of healthcare itemised on their payslips, patients are looking for value.

In those five years, GP surgeries become self-sustaining. No need for that £150 sweetener, and every incentive to get as many patients through the doors as they can. It's a great business to be in.

Already, the most innovative providers are getting entrepreneurial, with **technology**. Up next.

3. Innovate with technology

Babylon Health offers GP services, under the same NHS contract as your family doctor, to thousands in London and Birmingham. It's not a building—it's an app.

From your phone, Babylon offers an artificial intelligence chatbot for health advice, video consultations with human doctors, and face-to-face visits at a surgery in town. A complete GP service, with bells and whistles.

Sounds sci-fi? Nope. Expert systems have been diagnosing patients through decision-tree conversations—with greater success, on average, than a trained human doctor—since the 1980s. Doctors (correctly) realised such software represented a threat to their incomes, and fought their introduction for decades. Today's GP, more comfortable with technology, perhaps opposes them less.

So the next step is to ==encourage such software in surgeries==. (GPs are a £33bn chunk of NHS costs.) In other words, introduce the tech, without taking away the human face. This avoids ruffling the feathers of the biggest healthcare consumers, older people.

(A surprising amount of the time, all a young doctor's doing behind her keyboard is Googling your ailment anyway. What if for each £3 visit a patient could serve themselves at a PC in the waiting room?)

Let innovation shine. It's about time.

4. From tax to voucher

The next step in doing healthcare right is a bit of financial ju-jitsu. Keep on itemising that £2,000 on everyone's tax return . . . but start calling it a *voucher*.

Consumers can use that voucher to buy private health insurance. Even *comprehensive* health insurance, if they want, taking them out of public healthcare entirely. (Such insurance, today, costs a lot less than £2,000 a year.)

And it gives change. If their insurance costs £1,200, they get an £800 tax rebate. Whoopee!

This is, conservatively estimated, a £33bn sector waiting to happen.

Some might complain this takes resources away from public healthcare. Well, it reduces tax receipts, yes. **That's the point.** The goal is to turn pricey *public* healthcare into a profitable *private* industry, free of malign misincentives.

Yes, people have principles. But they also have their price. And a few years in, more relaxed about paying the odd £3 to see a doctor, the population might be more open to getting a little value back.

All this happens without changing any healthcare infrastructure, because the groundwork of shifting *mindsets* must come before shifting healthcare *models*. Let's say we're three years in, and it's time for that next stage.

5. From public cost to private provider

This cheaper, customer-focussed healthcare system hasn't undergone much structural change yet: it's still using GP surgeries, treatment centres, public hospitals. Here's the real beauty of our model for doing healthcare: *it doesn't have to.*

Most NHS hospitals sit in "trusts"—essentially, 150 self-governing groups of care providers. They can set their own budgets, attract their own patients (some are surprisingly entrepreneurial) and receive payment based on the number of patients and conditions trundling through the doors. Many function at a loss, but that's not the point here.

The action needed is to turn these quasi-businesses

into *real* businesses ... ==while still serving the same populations, in the same way==.

Even though it's now a private business, you'll still go to your local hospital. You'll still see the same nurses, doctors, bedpans. It's just that the hospital is now competing with others for your business—and those lucrative payments from your health insurer.

How will we persuade health workers to accept this change? Once again, we're inspired by the noble capitalist ethos of socialist politician and NHS founder, Nye Bevan.

A large hospital is a huge business asset: perhaps £1bn or more. If taken from self-governing trust to self-governing private business, that £1bn needs to go somewhere. Who gets it?

Answer: **the NHS staff themselves**.

Every consultant, doctor, nurse, and porter receives shares in the "company" his or her hospital has become. (Britain's John Lewis and Waitrose, employee-owned retailers, might provide a useful template.) Suddenly, that low-paid cleaner owns £20,000 of shares in her employer. And she deserves every penny.

By cleaning harder, she'll increase the *value* of those shares. By packing the operating theatre, a surgeon increases the value of *his* stash, maybe over £1m. Everyone—hell, maybe even the local community— shares in the bonanza, in proportion to their salaries.

(Yes, this is broad brush. But isn't it a great principle?)

People work harder and smarter when they have a stake in the enterprise they work for. And with a profit motive, the hospital can start improving—*really* improving, competing and innovating on market principles to attract customers and make profits.

And, of course, it can go bust.

But it starts with a huge advantage: it'll often be the main player in the community. In other words, the current monopoly holder. But now a *competitive* monopoly, no longer a coercive one.

With a profit motive and market forces stirred in, there's now an incentive for *other* players to start offering medical services to local residents. Which means those medics are going to start treating you as what you are.

Not a name to be crossed off. Not a number to be reached or a metric to be met. Not even a patient to be processed . . . but a *customer* to be *satisfied*.

When hospital managers realise they're sitting on a £1bn asset, they'll start sweating it. Like any other business owner.

A few more years in, this fulfils our fifth step: taking healthcare out of the government budget entirely. We've done it by creating a huge incentive for hospital staff. But there's one more point in our six-point plan: incentives for the *consumer*.

6. Consumer incentives

By this point, Britain's healthcare system is private, with the most obvious changes all positive. The public are using familiar hospitals, the same surgeons, the same GP . . . but they're getting better service, because they're no longer a captive audience. The transitional step of vouchers has disappeared from payslips; consumers now buy health insurance directly, able to afford it now tax bills are a lot lower. (Let's make health insurance premiums tax-deductible, just for fun. After all, the UK's now saving £120bn a year.)

The final step in the journey from a public sector healthcare system to a free-market one happens naturally, as hospitals and insurers compete for customers. It's about **rewarding the consumer**.

Let's go back to car insurance, and how claims are dealt with. Providers share information on incidents and accidents, and build up a history of your behaviour to decide how much they'll charge you.

Here's an idea: competing providers offer a **health score**, much like a credit score. (It's less about privacy than you think: you agree to have your details analysed by credit scoring companies whenever you apply for a credit card or bank account.) Points out of 1,000 map to the likelihood of you needing healthcare services; light users get offered lower premiums.

(Yes, smokers, drug addicts, and sexaholics will pay more. And why shouldn't they?)

And that's our six-point plan for doing healthcare right. We've missed a few stakeholder groups so far: shortly we'll address the issues of the unemployed, disabled, and those with pre-existing conditions.

First, a word on what makes this all work: **amortisation**.

THE AMORTISATION ISSUE

Playing yang to risk's yin is the other concept that makes insurance work: **amortisation**.

Your insurer can cover your £20,000 heart op on your £100 premium, because 100,000 other people are paying that £100 too. And statistically only a few will need heart surgery.

This is the area where today's health insurance *differs* from motor insurance.

Everyone with a car is legally compelled to take out insurance, and this large number of policyholders lets the insurer spread its risk and offer you a competitive price.

Yet in "private" healthcare markets like the USA, not everyone who has health (i.e. is alive) takes out health insurance. So people who'd normally spread the risk—young, healthy people who need little healthcare—aren't there to pool the risk, making premiums pricey.

(This happens a *lot*. Worsened further by a $280bn market distortion that offers tax deductibility to employers but not individuals.)

So to ensure there's enough of a pool for amortisation, the first step in turning inefficient socialised healthcare into competitive market-based healthcare is to make health insurance compulsory, much as car insurance is compulsory.

It isn't a very free-market solution—but it'd be temporary, just to cover the gap before the system becomes competitive enough to make having insurance the only sensible option.

To do healthcare right, compulsion is the hold-your-nose solution that smooths the transition between government-provided and market-based healthcare. And within this, there are ways to cover people from economically inactive groups, or those who need more healthcare through no fault of their own, such as disabled people. (More on these "edge cases" shortly.)

So for a transition period—5-10 years—our example here, the UK population, will be legally required to buy comprehensive health insurance. It's not very capitalist. But it'll get the party started.

A CHANGED UNDERSTANDING

So: the solution is an insurance model, covering the costs of healthcare, spread out among the population to amortise costs. Premiums everyone has to pay.

Some people argue that this sounds like taxes. (Hey, we're all in this together; we're all sharing the cost!) So it's no different to a government-provided system.

They couldn't be more wrong.

It's only "compulsory" in the same sense as car insurance: protection against risk for yourself and others' claims on you. Your health insurance isn't a gift to government at gunpoint; it's a payment to your preferred provider, in a free and open market.

And the whole point of this six-point plan—from itemising healthcare costs to rewarding staff with shares in their place of work—is to *make healthcare a competitive market*. To change public perception (our first Big Problem) by fostering the understanding that your health is in your hands. And take the biggest line item in government budgets—health—off the books, so the economy can become more competitive.

If your own health isn't important to you, why should you expect someone else to pay for it? Even a faceless government? This is the general issue with *all* government services: they abrogate personal responsibility in favour of a vague collectivism.

This is the toxic belief this little book tries to overcome. Because it's been around far too long.

THE TROUBLE WITH "PRIMARY CARE"

With that thought, let's talk *attitudes*.

Western healthcare has long been about fixing problems after the fact, rather than preventing them before they arise. It's the wrong mindset.

But you can still find the right one in traditional societies. In the jungles of South America and across Asia, **self-care**, body and mind, is where it starts. And they lead long and healthy lives. (If they can avoid being eaten by jaguars or tripping over a tree trunk.)

And in our free-market healthcare system, the value of establishing and maintaining your *own* health will be clear. Your clean-living self will get lower premiums than Marlboro Martin down the boozer, whose idea of a balanced diet is alternating KFC with McDonalds.

The worst example of the current mindset in the UK is the bureaucratese for family doctor: *Primary Carer*.

Because doctors are secondary. Your primary carer is *yourself*.

And the deeper that thought spreads among the population, the healthier people will be.

So perhaps, with this changed mindset, there'll be a bonus: a healthier nation. And despite this book offering a market-based, capitalism-driven solution, there's no outcome more civic-minded than that.

CURING THOSE WITHOUT MONEY

In a free-market healthcare sector, prices will be competitive (because that's what free markets do). With products and services constantly improving. And with a huge line item taken out of government expenditure, taxes will be lower, allowing people to keep more of their incomes and make more spending decisions for themselves.

But not everyone *has* an income. For some, this is their own fault (and their own problem). But what about the genuinely incapacitated: those living in poverty, born or made disabled, the mentally ill, those in the last chapter of life?

This is an understandable (if misguided) complaint

against capitalism: that those without the resources to take part will get left behind.

So let's deal with it, case by case. How does this system work for those who can't afford it . . . yet perhaps need it most?

But first, another word on charity.

RETURNING CHARITY TO ITS ROOTS

As previously mentioned, hospitals, as customer-serving market players, should not have charitable status. But this *doesn't* mean there's no role for charities at all.

The role of charity is to <mark>help people in need</mark>. And community organisations, benevolent associations, and foundations have been helping the needy for millennia.

So there's nothing to stop newly-private NHS hospitals continuing their social mission by treating nonpayers, to maintain a tip-top reputation in the local community. In a free market, that's their choice. (Of course, it may affect the value of their shares in the hospital.)

And the next few pages will illustrate just how *few* people are "truly needy" in a market-based healthcare system. That number will never be zero. But it's lower than you think.

Charitable status is endlessly abused today: supposedly public-spirited enterprises build coercive monopolies and pay millions to CEOs, with a startling percentage of donations going to "overhead". (Aka: keeping it for themselves.)

A market-based system whisks aside the curtain, and forces charities to return to their roots: ==giving money to people who need it.==

To put in some numbers: Britain's top 1,000

charities disburse over £18bn each year. Paying for comprehensive health insurance for all 8m people in "absolute poverty", man, woman, and child, would cost less than half that figure.

And it's not even as pricey as *that*. Let's look next at that "absolute poverty" definition.

Paying for the poor

There are winners and losers in a capitalist economy: no point pretending otherwise. But also: there aren't as many *truly* penniless people as you think. (Any more than there are as many truly *wealthy* people as you think.)

So let's quantify "absolute poverty". In the UK, that's someone living at or below 60% of median household income: £29,400 * 0.6 = £17,640.

By this definition, 17% of UK households live in absolute poverty. Yet the idea these people are somehow one step away from living on the streets is **wrong**. (Some 50% of this group *own their own homes*.) It's one hell of a hardship budget, yes. But it'll still put a roof over your head and food on the table in many parts of the UK. And that makes you a *consumer*.

In fact, low-income households are *avid* consumers. And all sorts of businesses have succeeded by making their difficult lives a little brighter. Contract-free phones. Low-cost financing. Car auctions. Beauty salons. Sports clubs. Discount supermarkets. And a thousand more.

Healthcare, as this little book stresses repeatedly, is *not* different to other businesses. It is a professional service. And in a competitive market, the most profitable ventures are often those addressing large yet underserved niches.

Africa and Asia, again, are a source of ideas. From

Kenya's pay-by-phone innovations to India's cheap private schools to Bangladesh's microlenders, entrepreneurs have found ways to bring high-quality services to the poorest people, driven by the profit incentive.

That's what the market does. It solves hard things creatively. And the bigger the market, the bigger the economic incentive to serve it. So the market *will* find a way to offer health insurance to many of the 8m people in "absolute poverty".

Looks like that £18bn in charity handouts will be plenty to go around. (Assuming it hasn't all gone on "overhead".)

Dealing with disabilities

Charity **Scope** claims the UK has 14m disabled people. That's on the high side. (A disability charity has an incentive to highball, after all.) But it also mentions their 92% employment rate (higher than the *total* rate in France, Spain, or Greece) and their £249bn in annual household spending.

So the differently-abled are anything but a burden on society. Many disabled people work very hard; many hold fulltime jobs; many are as productive as any able-bodied individual.

The disabled aren't objects of pity. They're functioning people, to be celebrated. So there's no reason to discriminate against disabled people when it comes to health insurance.

Yes, a market-based system means higher premiums. Charities will jump to subsidise these. (*If they're genuine charities, and not, say, private businesses in disguise*). But more to the point, the disabled demographic is a *market opportunity*.

Innovative prosthetics. Redesigned housing. Ergonomic furniture. What if innovative financing and insurance policies could cover *these*, and do so profitably, without the whiff of good-enough-for-government-work?

That's the great thing about markets. People are customers, not burdens.

Providing for pre-existing

A similar challenge to those with disabilities are people with pre-existing conditions. (In fact, there's a lot of overlap.)

In a free-market healthcare system, the knowledge of ongoing costs means higher insurance prices: no way around it. But greater knowledge always leads to *more* price competition, not less.

So in a truly free market—where all risk can be accurately priced, not inflated by laws that outlaw evidence about gender, genetics, and lifestyle—there *will* be premiums supporting pre-existing conditions at reasonable cost.

Furthermore, a great many pre-existing conditions aren't lifelong. Western healthcare's great bugbear, obesity, is reversible if there's an incentive to do so. When it costs them an extra £250 a month, you might be surprised to see fewer feckless fatties around town.

Again, market forces balance things out. And with 66m people in the UK, there's a big enough pool of risk to amortise them all.

Solving for the psyche

Mental illness is corrosive. It slows productive work; it reduces opportunities; it prevents full functioning in society. In short, it's an ailment like any other.

There should be no stigma about it: the brain is just another organ. And it can get broken just the same.

But sufferers have a very hard time, because all too often it's invisible. And many insurance policies don't cover mental conditions.

Hey, that sounds like an underserved market. *Great!* In a free market, there'll be a range of cover that prices your risk of mental illness correctly. Even better: with a profit incentive, treatment options will broaden too.

Caring for the crinklies

Harking back to Big Problem 3 again, the average UK citizen suffers seven years of ill health towards the end of life. Over-65s suck in 40% of the NHS's total budget, and they're just 18% of the population.

So . . . twice the spend. Maybe twice the premium. Is that *really* so unaffordable?

Across the UK, disposable income for the over-65s is growing twice as fast as those in younger brackets. With mortgages paid off and children grown up, demands on income are lower in any case.

Far from a needy group, pensioners are a profitable demographic. (UK charities Saga and Age Concern even promote insurance policies specifically *aimed* at these lucky oldies, despite the amortisation issue.)

So with risk correctly priced and amortisation providing a broad pool, it's unlikely private healthcare policies will be unaffordable for the Werther's Originals brigade. Indeed, the UK's tiny private health insurance sector (just £350m) works well already, and its policyholders trend older.

(*Social* care, such as residential, is a larger problem, but it's one of income, not healthcare. Look for the next book, "How to do Welfare".)

Pensioners aren't a disadvantaged group. They are, however, an underserved one. Let the free market serve them.

COUNTING THE OUTLIERS

These five edge cases—the old, the low-paid, the disabled, those with pre-existing conditions and the mentally ill—illustrate how outliers, in a free and open market, are simply part of the diversity and variation that keep society interesting.

In other words, they're part of the **Normal Distribution**: that ol' bell-shaped curve.

In any question about risk and amortisation, a Normal Distribution can settle most arguments. It provides two bits of data: the mean (μ) and the Standard Deviation (σ). The mean is where healthy adults cluster: Mr and Ms Average. While the SD tells you how far your outliers are *from* that mean.

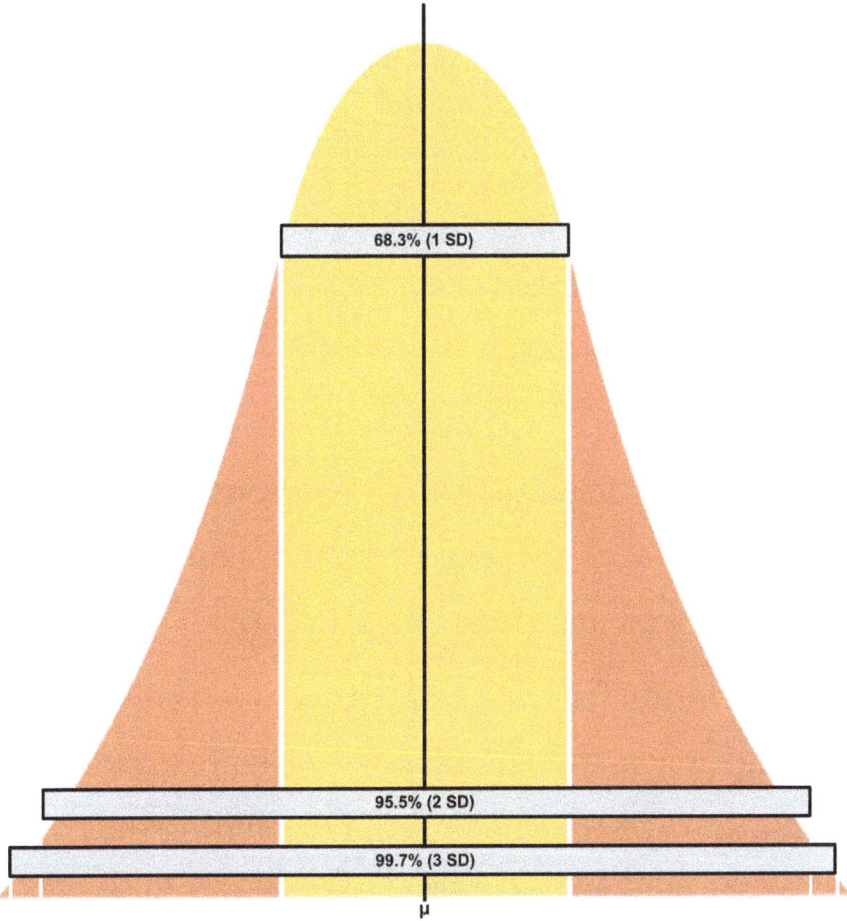

68.3% (1 SD)

95.5% (2 SD)

99.7% (3 SD)

μ

These averagely healthy folk take up the 68.3% around the mean ("within one SD"). Another 27.2%, split into two halves of less healthy and unusually well, fill it out on each side to 95.5%, or 2 SDs. And a smaller proportion, 4.2%, take coverage to 99.7%. (In this third SD, 2.1% are always at the doc's and half can't even remember when they last needed one.)

(Why distribute data this way? Because you see these percentages in ecosystems and economies all the time: they're an unofficial law of nature.)

A illustration for our healthcare model: general insurance covers the first SD, specialist insurance the second, and at 3 SDs and beyond (including that tiny 0.3% at the edges, the 0.15% of people with huge healthcare needs) **charity** steps in, helping that 2.25%

of people who (for no fault of their own) are outside population norms.

In a capitalist economy, the Normal Distribution of a population is its risk pool: your mathematical model of the total market pie. Without the skews and kinks introduced in a government system.

Now for a few head-scratchers for the capitalist approach: **vaccines**, **pregnancy**, and the **emergency room**.

EVALUATING VACCINES

Despite the sad efforts of a few idiotic miserabilists to prove otherwise, **vaccines work**. They're about the greatest medical success story since handwashing.

Yet the jabs are stabbed in early life, *before* the child becomes that ultimate prize, a **consumer**. This might seem problematic for anything market-based. (Babies don't have big bank balances.)

It's really not. Vaccines save vast amounts of money in later-life medical care. Which means there's an incentive to offer cheaper premiums to parents who vaccinate their kids. As always, money talks.

That's all we need to do on vaccines.

CORNERING KIDS

There's one medical procedure that happens to up to half the population at some point despite being completely healthy: **pregnancy**.

Planned or otherwise, it's a medical matter. And since it's optional, the free market would state the costs are on you. (They can be high. In the USA it starts around $20,000.)

It's good to have children. The human race is screwed if we don't. (With birthrates far below replacement rate in Japan, Italy, and elsewhere, we may be screwed anyway.) So: how can health insurance cover it?

By looking ahead.

Insurance works on probabilities. Statistically, your 15-year old daughter will give birth 1.6 times between now and 45. Caught early, that's an easy factor to price into coverage.

"Pregnancy insurance" sounds a sinister thing for any father to take out for his daughter. But in reality it's a deeply positive thing. So even in a fully private market focussing on rare, ruinous, and hard-to-predict events, there are options for covering the costs of the greatest *predictable* event in life.

THE A&E DILEMMA

The thorniest problem in healthcare is that "red room" awash in blood and vomit, known in the UK as Accident and Emergency, and in the USA as the emergency room.

Concepts like amortisation and risk spreading are harder to apply to A&E. It has to be ready for anything, from one crying child to a busload of bleeding bodies on the motorway. Weekly boom-and-bust cycles (the Friday night binge drinking club) clog up the system, with the urgent cases coming in right as the best people go off duty.

And no doctor is going to ask a mangled victim for his health insurance details.

So how can private healthcare make a profit from the emergency room?

It can't.

Well, *maybe* it can't.

Because its unpredictable workload breaks the insurance model, emergency care is, perhaps, the one gap capitalism can't close. But who knows?

In a population with 95% coverage, there's enough of a chance your patient is covered to make treatment less of a financial risk. And with 24m A&E visits in the UK last year, it's a big enough market for *some* bright ideas to arise in.

So we *could* have private A&E providers. But for now, this is an open question.

THERE'S SOME SICK PEOPLE OUT THERE

So how long would it take to execute this six-point plan and solve our three Big Problems of healthcare?

A minimum of five years. Realistically, ten. Perhaps even a generation. But that's okay.

Because as long as it provides incremental improvements at each step, without leaving people behind, it's fulfilling its objectives.

Government treats those millions of patients as a problem to be solved. The market sees them as an *opportunity*. And where opportunities exist, innovative ideas blossom.

Finally, a word to the medical professionals.

PHYSICIAN, HEAL THYSELF

Some might say we can't afford to change our basic model of healthcare. The truth: we can't afford not to.

Costs are rising beyond inflation, beyond incomes. Usage is rising, too. Britain's NHS is short of 100,000 workers. (After the Brexit referendum, applications from Europe for nursing posts fell 96%.)

Because you can't attract people into professions by passing laws and setting quotas. You attract them with *incentives*.

And in a free market, one doctor making a large profit is an incentive to compete and make those profits yourself. Over time, that first doctor finds he has competitors. And prices for consumers go down, as those doctors compete and innovate to attract and retain customers.

So an addendum to our six-point plan is a message to physicians: <mark>stop being compliant in the system</mark>. Stop relying on governments to train you, find you jobs, fill your pockets, pay your pension.

A competitive capitalist healthcare sector offers you more opportunities, greater wealth, and the chance to deliver better patient satisfaction than ever before.

The market provides. Embrace its opportunities.

And that's how to do healthcare.

ABOUT CHRIS

Chris Worth is a London-based copywriter and author of the guide to effective freelancing **100 Days, 100 Grand**. Google it or head for 100days100grand.com.

At work, he creates campaigns and content backed by meaningful insights, mostly for technology clients. (He does the research and analysis too, btw—his USP.)

Interests include adventure travel and extreme sports. He's lived in six countries, visited 60, and is a qualified sky *and* scuba diver with a passion for calisthenics and kettlebells. But he's never without his Kindle. See him at chrisdoescontent.com.

www.ingramcontent.com/pod-product-compliance
Lightning Source LLC
Chambersburg PA
CBHW081820200326

41597CB00023B/4321